Retro Revival

Rediscovering the Best Abandonware Games of the 80s & 90s

By Corey Harris

"Journey through pixels and memory lanes, where the heart of gaming's golden age remains - an odyssey of forgotten realms and digital dreams."

Copyright © 2023

Table of Contents

Dedication

To the visionary game developers of the past, whose ingenuity laid the foundation of virtual worlds, and to the gamers of the future, who will continue to explore and expand these realms. This book is a bridge between generations, celebrating the legacy that connects us all.

1.Introduction to Abandonware

Definition and Legal Considerations

Abandonware refers to software, particularly video games, that is no longer sold or supported by its publisher. This term typically applies to games from the 1980s and 1990s that are no longer available on the market due to various reasons such as business closures, outdated technology, or lost copyrights. While abandonware is often freely available online, its legal status remains a gray area. The copyright for these games often still exists, making their distribution without permission technically a violation of copyright laws. However, due to the lack of enforcement or interest from the copyright holders, many of these games have slipped into a realm of tacit allowance, where they are downloaded and played by enthusiasts without major legal repercussions.

The Cultural Impact of 80s and 90s Games

The games of the 80s and 90s laid the foundation for modern video gaming. They introduced groundbreaking concepts in storytelling, gameplay mechanics, and visual design. Titles from this era, such as "The Legend of Zelda," "Doom," and "SimCity," not only shaped the gaming industry but also left a lasting impact on popular culture. They influenced a generation of gamers, developers, and artists, inspiring creativity and innovation in various fields. The simplicity and originality of these games often evoke nostalgia, reminding players of a time when gameplay and imagination were paramount.

The Resurgence of Retro Gaming

In recent years, there's been a significant resurgence in retro gaming. This revival is driven partly by nostalgia and partly by a desire to experience gaming history. Modern gamers, intrigued by the origins of the industry, turn to these classic games to understand the evolution of gaming. Furthermore, the rise of digital platforms and emulators has made accessing these old games easier than ever. This resurgence isn't just about playing old games; it's about preserving and appreciating the rich history of the medium. Retro gaming events, online communities, and re-releases of classic consoles have become increasingly popular, highlighting the timeless appeal of these pioneering games.

2. The Dawn of Digital Gaming: Key Innovations of the 1980s

Pioneering Games and Genres

The 1980s were a transformative period for digital gaming, marked by the introduction of numerous groundbreaking games and the establishment of enduring genres. This era saw the birth of iconic titles like "Pac-Man," "Tetris," and "Super Mario Bros.," each representing different genres – arcade, puzzle, and platformer, respectively. These games not only defined their genres but also set standards for game design that are still relevant today. "Pac-Man" introduced the concept of power-ups and non-linear gameplay, "Tetris" showcased the addictive nature of simple yet challenging puzzle mechanics, and "Super Mario Bros." revolutionized platform gaming with its smooth scrolling and precise control.

Technological Breakthroughs in Gaming

The 80s were also a time of significant technological innovation in gaming. The introduction of 8-bit systems like the Nintendo Entertainment System (NES) and the Commodore 64 brought about a dramatic improvement in game graphics and sound. This advancement allowed for more complex and visually appealing games, fostering a more immersive gaming experience. The era also saw the evolution of home computer gaming, with platforms like the Apple II and the IBM PC offering new opportunities for game development. These technological strides were instrumental in moving gaming from simple, monochrome experiences to richer, more engaging adventures.

Profile: Iconic Game Developers of the 80s

Several game developers left an indelible mark on the 1980s, pioneering new approaches to game design and storytelling. Shigeru Miyamoto, the creator of Mario and The Legend of Zelda, stands out for his innovative design philosophy that combined simple, intuitive gameplay with rich worlds and characters. Richard Garriott, with his Ultima series, introduced many to the possibilities of role-playing games, blending storytelling with player choice and character development. Sid Meier, another notable figure, began his journey with titles like "Pirates!" and "Civilization," laying the groundwork for strategy and simulation games. These developers not only created enjoyable games but also pushed the boundaries of what video games could be, influencing countless others in the industry.

3. The 90s: A Decade of Gaming Evolution

Graphical Advancements and Gameplay Innovations

The 1990s represented a quantum leap in the world of video gaming, primarily through remarkable graphical advancements and gameplay innovations. This decade witnessed the transition from 2D to 3D graphics, a monumental shift that changed how games were played and experienced. The introduction of 3D graphics with consoles like the Sony PlayStation and the Nintendo 64 allowed for a more immersive and realistic gaming environment. Games like "Super Mario 64" and "Tomb Raider" showcased this evolution, offering players expansive 3D worlds to explore. This era also saw the refinement of genres like first-person shooters (FPS), with titles like "Doom" and "Half-Life" setting benchmarks for immersive gameplay and level design. In terms of gameplay, this period experimented with complex mechanics, including real-time strategy in games like "StarCraft" and intricate puzzle-solving in "Myst." These innovations not only enhanced the gaming experience but also expanded the medium's appeal to a broader audience.

The Rise of Complex Storytelling in Games

The 90s also marked the rise of complex storytelling in video games. This was the era when narrative and character development became as crucial as gameplay. Role-playing games (RPGs) like "Final Fantasy VII" and "Baldur's Gate" offered deep, intricate stories that could rival traditional media like books and films. These narratives were often characterized by epic quests, moral choices, and character development, providing a much more immersive and emotionally engaging experience. Adventure games such as "The Secret of Monkey Island" and "Grim Fandango" brought in witty writing, humor, and well-crafted plots, showing that games could be both entertaining and intellectually stimulating. The integration of cinematic elements, including cutscenes and voice acting, further enhanced the storytelling, allowing players to connect with characters and the game world on a deeper level.

Memorable Game Soundtracks and Audio

The 1990s were also a golden era for game soundtracks and audio design. Advances in audio technology allowed for more complex and dynamic soundscapes, which played a significant role in the gaming experience. Iconic soundtracks from games like "The Legend of Zelda: Ocarina of Time" and "Chrono Trigger" were not only memorable but also emotionally resonant, enhancing the narrative and setting the tone of the game. The use of voice acting became more prevalent, with games like "Metal Gear Solid" using it to add depth to characters and storytelling. Ambient sounds and audio cues in games like "Resident Evil" were used effectively to build atmosphere and tension. The audio advancements of this era were critical in transforming games into a more holistic sensory experience, engaging players on multiple levels.

4. Adventure and Role-Playing Games

Notable Titles and Their Lasting Influence

Adventure and role-playing games (RPGs) have been pivotal in the evolution of video gaming, offering immersive worlds, deep storytelling, and complex character development. The 80s and 90s were especially significant for these genres, as they saw the release of numerous titles that would leave an enduring legacy.

The Adventure of Link and the Rise of Action RPGs: The late 1980s witnessed a significant shift with the release of "The Legend of Zelda: The Adventure of Link." This game blended traditional RPG elements like experience points and a leveling system with real-time combat, setting a precedent for action RPGs. Its open-world exploration and non-linear gameplay encouraged exploration and experimentation, elements that would become staples in later RPGs.

Final Fantasy and the Art of Storytelling: The "Final Fantasy" series, starting from its inception in 1987, played a monumental role in popularizing RPGs worldwide. With its intricate plots, well-developed characters, and turn-based combat system, Final Fantasy set a high standard for storytelling in games. Each installment introduced new mechanics and narrative techniques, pushing the boundaries of what could be achieved in video game storytelling. For instance, "Final Fantasy VI" introduced multiple storylines and a large ensemble cast, while "Final Fantasy VII" became renowned for its cinematic presentation and deep, emotionally charged narrative.

Chrono Trigger's Innovations: "Chrono Trigger," released in 1995, was another landmark title. It was celebrated for its innovative gameplay features, like multiple endings and a combat system that combined turn-based and real-time elements. The game's plot, involving time travel, allowed for a diverse range of settings and narrative possibilities, making each player's journey unique. Its approach to storytelling, where player choices had significant consequences, influenced numerous RPGs that followed.

Baldur's Gate and Western RPGs: The late 90s saw the rise of Western RPGs, with "Baldur's Gate" (1998) being a standout example. This game brought the depth of Dungeons & Dragons to computer RPGs, featuring a vast, interactive world and a complex morality system. It emphasized character customization and strategic combat, elements that would become central to Western RPG design.

Diablo and the Dungeon Crawling Genre: "Diablo," released in 1996, revolutionized the RPG genre with its fast-paced action and randomly generated dungeons. It introduced the concept of looting and grinding for better equipment, a mechanic that became fundamental in many RPGs and action games thereafter. The game's multiplayer feature also set a new standard for cooperative gameplay in RPGs.

The evolution of adventure and role-playing games (RPGs) in the 80s and 90s was not just about the titles themselves, but also about the innovative mechanics and narrative techniques they introduced. These elements collectively transformed the gaming landscape, setting new benchmarks for interactive storytelling and gameplay.

Choice and Consequence: One of the most significant narrative techniques introduced in RPGs was the concept of player choice impacting the game's story and outcome. Games like "Baldur's Gate" and "Fallout" offered branching storylines and multiple endings based on players' decisions, lending a sense of agency and personal investment in the narrative. This approach allowed for more dynamic and personalized storytelling, making each playthrough unique.

Character Customization and Development: RPGs of this era greatly expanded on character customization, allowing players to tailor their characters' abilities, appearances, and backstories. This level of personalization enabled players to immerse themselves more deeply in the game world. Games like "Diablo" and "The Elder Scrolls" series offered extensive skill trees and equipment options, giving players a sense of growth and progression as their characters evolved.

World Building and Exploration: The creation of rich, detailed game worlds was another hallmark of these genres. Titles such as "The Legend of Zelda" and "Final Fantasy" series crafted expansive universes with their own histories, cultures, and geographies. This depth encouraged exploration and discovery, making the game world an integral part of the overall experience.

Integration of Puzzles and Quests: Adventure games, in particular, were known for their clever integration of puzzles and quests. Games like "Monkey Island" and "Myst" featured intricate puzzles that were not just challenges to be overcome but also narrative devices that advanced the story and enriched the game world.

Narrative Depth and Emotional Engagement: The storytelling in these games started to rival that of traditional media, with complex plots, well-rounded characters, and emotional depth. Games like "Chrono Trigger" and "Final Fantasy VII" were notable for their epic narratives, which dealt with themes like friendship, sacrifice, and the struggle against destiny. These stories resonated with players, creating emotional connections that lasted well beyond the gameplay.

Use of Cinematics: The use of cinematic cutscenes became increasingly popular as a way to advance the story and develop characters. Games like "Metal Gear Solid" and "Final Fantasy" series used cinematics to create dramatic, movie-like experiences, blending gameplay with storytelling in a seamless manner.

Comprehensive List of Adventure and Role-Playing Games (80s to Early 90s)

1. **The Legend of Zelda (1986)** - A groundbreaking adventure game introducing the fantasy world of Hyrule.

2. **Final Fantasy (1987)** - This RPG set a new standard for storytelling and gameplay in the genre.

3. **Dragon Warrior (Dragon Quest) (1986)** - Pioneered many RPG elements with its fantasy setting.

4. **Ultima IV: Quest of the Avatar (1985)** - Known for its deep morality system and open world.

5. **King's Quest I: Quest for the Crown (1984, Sierra Online)** - A trendsetter in graphical adventure gaming.

6. **Phantasy Star (1987)** - A seminal RPG combining sci-fi elements with traditional fantasy.

7. **Maniac Mansion (1987)** - A revolutionary adventure game with a unique multi-character control system.

8. **Space Quest I: The Sarien Encounter (1986, Sierra Online)** - Blended humor with sci-fi in a memorable adventure.

9. **The Secret of Monkey Island (1990)** - A defining game in the genre with its pirate theme and humor.

10. **Pool of Radiance (1988)** - A D&D-based RPG, praised for its tactical depth.

11. **Leisure Suit Larry in the Land of the Lounge Lizards (1987, Sierra Online)** - A comedic, adult-themed adventure.

12. **Quest for Glory I: So You Want to Be a Hero (1989, Sierra Online)** - Combined RPG elements with adventure gaming.

13. **Gold Rush! (1988, Sierra Online)** - Known for its historical setting and branching narratives.

14. **Shadowgate (1987)** - A fantasy adventure game that stood out for its challenging puzzles.

15. **Wasteland (1988)** - A post-apocalyptic RPG that influenced many future games.

16. **Police Quest: In Pursuit of the Death Angel (1987, Sierra Online)** - Offered a realistic police procedural experience.

17. **Loom (1990)** - Featured a unique musical puzzle system and a compelling story.

18. **Might and Magic Book One: The Secret of the Inner Sanctum (1986)** - An RPG famous for its expansive world.

19. **Conquests of Camelot: The Search for the Grail (1990, Sierra Online)** - Mixed Arthurian legend with adventure gaming.

20. **Zak McKracken and the Alien Mindbenders (1988)** - A humorous take on sci-fi tropes.

21. **Wizardry: Proving Grounds of the Mad Overlord (1981)** - One of the first games to popularize the RPG genre.

22. **Gabriel Knight: Sins of the Fathers (1993, Sierra Online)** - A deep narrative-driven supernatural mystery.

23. **Eye of the Beholder (1991)** - A dungeon crawler RPG known for its immersive gameplay.

24. **The Bard's Tale (1985)** - Combined challenging gameplay with a rich fantasy narrative.

25. **Tales of the Unknown: Volume I - The Bard's Tale (1985)** - Brought a new level of graphical detail to RPGs.

26. **Chrono Trigger (1995)** - A genre-defining RPG known for its time-traveling story and multiple endings.

27. **Indiana Jones and the Fate of Atlantis (1992)** - Combined adventure gaming with a beloved franchise.

28. **The Elder Scrolls: Arena (1994)** - An expansive open-world RPG setting the stage for future games in the series.

29. **Sierra's Quest for Glory II: Trial by Fire (1990)** - Blended puzzle-solving with a rich narrative.

30. **Dungeon Master (1987)** - A real-time RPG that was revolutionary for its time.

31. **Mother (Earthbound Zero) (1989)** - A unique RPG with a modern setting and quirky humor.

32. **Full Throttle (1995)** - A narrative-driven adventure game set in a dystopian future.

33. **Monkey Island 2: LeChuck's Revenge (1991)** - Continued the humorous pirate adventures of its predecessor.

34. **Day of the Tentacle (1993)** - A time-traveling, puzzle-filled adventure game with a comedic twist.

35. **Sam & Max Hit the Road (1993)** - Featured a comedic duo in a whimsical adventure.

36. **The Illusion of Gaia (1993)** - An action RPG known for its story and puzzle elements.

37. **Sierra's King's Quest V: Absence Makes the Heart Go Yonder! (1990)** - Advanced the series with improved graphics and sound.

38. **Grim Fandango (1998)** - A critically acclaimed adventure game with a unique art style.

39. **Star Control II (1992)** - Combined adventure with space exploration and combat.

40. **Alone in the Dark (1992)** - A pioneer in the survival horror genre with adventure elements.

41. **Secret of Mana (1993)** - An action RPG with a real-time battle system and cooperative gameplay.

42. **Sierra's Space Quest III: The Pirates of Pestulon (1989)** - A space adventure with humor and puzzles.

43. **Deja Vu (1985)** - A noir adventure game with a unique interface and detective story.

44. **Ultima VII: The Black Gate (1992)** - Known for its deep story and rich open world.

45. **Betrayal at Krondor (1993)** - A narrative-driven RPG set in a detailed fantasy world.

46. **Lands of Lore: The Throne of Chaos (1993)** - Combined traditional RPG elements with a rich narrative.

47. **Sierra's Hero's Quest: So You Want to Be a Hero (1989)** - An innovative mix of adventure and RPG mechanics.

48. **Beneath a Steel Sky (1994)** - A cyberpunk adventure known for its story and setting.

49. **Simon the Sorcerer (1993)** - Featured a humorous take on fantasy adventure tropes.

50. **Sierra's Leisure Suit Larry 3: Passionate Patti in Pursuit of the Pulsating Pectorals (1989)** - Continued the adult-themed comedic adventures of Larry.

5. Arcade-Style and Platform Games

The Transition from Arcades to Home Computers

The arcade era of the 1980s marked a significant period in gaming history, characterized by the popularity of coin-operated machines and the emergence of iconic titles. However, as the decade progressed, there was a notable shift as these arcade experiences began transitioning to home computers and consoles. This shift was fueled by several factors, including the rising cost of arcade machines, the convenience of playing games at home, and the rapid advancements in home computing technology.

Initially, home versions of arcade games often faced limitations due to less powerful hardware, leading to games that were similar in spirit but different in execution. However, as technology advanced, home computers and consoles like the Commodore 64, the Nintendo Entertainment System (NES), and the Sega Genesis began to more closely replicate, and sometimes even surpass, the arcade experience. This transition was significant as it democratized gaming, making it more accessible and allowing for a broader audience.

The move to home gaming also meant that developers began tailoring their designs to suit this new environment. Unlike arcades, where the focus was on short, intense gameplay sessions to maximize coin usage, home games began to emphasize longer, more in-depth experiences. This change paved the way for more complex game designs, narratives, and the rise of genres that thrived in a home setting, such as RPGs and adventure games.

Evolution of Platform Game Design

Platform games, a genre popularized by arcade hits like "Donkey Kong," underwent a significant evolution during this transition. The early platformers were simple, focusing on moving a character across different platforms while avoiding obstacles. However, with the move to home gaming, the genre began to evolve in complexity and creativity.

The release of "Super Mario Bros." in 1985 marked a turning point for platform games. It introduced elements such as scrolling levels, power-ups, and a narrative context, setting a new standard for the genre. This game's success spawned numerous imitators and innovators, leading to a golden age of platform gaming.

Throughout the late '80s and early '90s, platform games continued to evolve. Titles like "Sonic the Hedgehog" introduced speed and attitude, appealing to a slightly older demographic, while games like "Prince of Persia" brought in more realistic animations and complex storytelling. The platform genre also began to branch out with the introduction of isometric platformers like "Q*bert" and puzzle-platformers like "Lemmings," which blended traditional platform mechanics with puzzle-solving elements.

This era also saw the introduction of mascot characters, with many platform games featuring a character that would become the face of the console or company. These mascots, like Mario for Nintendo and Sonic for Sega, became cultural icons and played a significant role in the marketing and identity of gaming platforms.

Great Arcade-Style and Platform Games (80s to Early 90s)

1. **Donkey Kong (1981)** - An early platformer that introduced the world to Mario, originally named Jumpman.

2. **Super Mario Bros. (1985)** - Revolutionized platform gaming with smooth scrolling and precise control.

3. **Pac-Man (1980)** - A maze arcade game that became a cultural icon with its simple yet addictive gameplay.

4. **Space Invaders (1978)** - Pioneered the shooter genre and set the template for future arcade games.

5. **Sonic the Hedgehog (1991)** - Known for its fast-paced gameplay and the introduction of Sega's mascot.

6. **Prince of Persia (1989)** - Brought fluid character animations and complex storytelling to platformers.

7. **Mega Man (1987)** - Combined platforming with run-and-gun elements and introduced a unique power-up system.

8. **Castlevania (1986)** - Known for its gothic themes and challenging platforming and combat mechanics.

9. **Galaga (1981)** - A popular space shooter that built upon the foundations set by Space Invaders.

10. **Bubble Bobble (1986)** - A platformer famous for its cooperative gameplay and cute characters.

11. **Duck Hunt (1984)** - An early example of a light gun shooter, remembered for its simplicity and fun.

12. **Tetris (1984)** - A tile-matching puzzle game that became one of the best-selling games of all time.

13. **Contra (1987)** - Known for its tough run-and-gun gameplay and the infamous "Konami Code."

14. **Street Fighter II (1991)** - Revolutionized the fighting game genre with its character variety and combo system.

15. **Double Dragon (1987)** - One of the first successful examples of the beat 'em up genre.

16. **Kirby's Dream Land (1992)** - Introduced the world to Kirby, known for its simplicity and innovative gameplay.

17. **Metal Slug (1996)** - A run-and-gun shooter known for its detailed animations and humor.

18. **Frogger (1981)** - A classic arcade game that challenged players to navigate a frog across busy roads and rivers.

19. **Out Run (1986)** - A groundbreaking driving game known for its fast-paced gameplay and branching paths.

20. **Q*bert (1982)** - An isometric platformer with a unique premise and challenging gameplay.

21. **Ghosts 'n Goblins (1985)** - Renowned for its high difficulty and spooky, atmospheric levels.

22. **Pitfall! (1982)** - One of the earliest platformers, it set many standards for the genre.

23. **Altered Beast (1988)** - A beat 'em up famous for its transformation sequences and mythical themes.

24. **Mortal Kombat (1992)** - Gained notoriety for its realistic graphics and brutal finishing moves.

25. **Bomberman (1983)** - A strategic, maze-based game known for its multiplayer mode.

26. **R-Type (1987)** - A side-scrolling shooter known for its difficulty and unique power-up system.

27. **The Legend of Zelda (1986)** - Though not a traditional platformer, it influenced many action-adventure games.

28. **Teenage Mutant Ninja Turtles: The Arcade Game (1989)** - A popular beat 'em up based on the animated series.

29. **Final Fight (1989)** - Helped popularize the beat 'em up genre with its large sprites and cooperative gameplay.

30. **Ikari Warriors (1986)** - A run-and-gun shooter that allowed simultaneous two-player action.

31. **Dig Dug (1982)** - A maze arcade game where players inflate and destroy enemies.

32. **Pong (1972)** - One of the earliest arcade games, it laid the foundation for video games as a whole.

33. **Asteroids (1979)** - A space-themed shooter that became one of the most popular games of its time.

34. **Centipede (1980)** - A fixed shooter where players defend against centipedes, spiders, and other creatures.

35. **Defender (1980)** - A side-scrolling shooter known for its fast-paced gameplay and complexity.

36. **Missile Command (1980)** - A strategy shooter where players defend cities from a barrage of missiles.

37. **Joust (1982)** - Featured unique gameplay where players joust against enemies on flying ostriches.

38. **Robotron: 2084 (1982)** - A twin-stick shooter known for its frantic gameplay and high difficulty.

39. **Berzerk (1980)** - A multi-directional shooter set in a maze filled with robots.

40. **Moon Patrol (1982)** - Combined side-scrolling shooting with driving, known for its parallax scrolling.

41. **Marble Madness (1984)** - An innovative game where players navigate a marble through intricate 3D courses.

42. **Paperboy (1984)** - A unique game where players control a paperboy delivering newspapers.

43. **Rampage (1986)** - Players control giant monsters to destroy cities, a hit in both arcades and home consoles.

44. **Track & Field (1983)** - A sports-themed game that tested players' speed and reflexes in various events.

45. **Tempest (1981)** - A tube shooter with unique graphics and gameplay mechanics.

46. **BurgerTime (1982)** - A platformer where players assemble burgers while avoiding enemies.

47. **Zaxxon (1982)** - Introduced isometric graphics in a shooter, offering a unique 3D perspective.

48. **Gauntlet (1985)** - A multiplayer dungeon crawl game known for its cooperative play.

49. **Spy Hunter (1983)** - A driving game where players control a spy car equipped with weapons.

50. **Excitebike (1984)** - A motocross racing game that allowed players to create their own tracks.

6. Strategy and Simulation Games

The Rise of Real-Time and Turn-Based Strategy

The late 1980s and early 1990s marked a significant era for strategy games, particularly with the emergence and refinement of real-time and turn-based strategy (RTS and TBS) genres. This period saw the development of games that not only challenged players' tactical skills but also their ability to manage resources and plan ahead in real-time or turn-based environments.

Turn-Based Strategy's Evolution: TBS games, like the "Civilization" series, which began in 1991, offered players the challenge of building and managing an empire through different historical periods. These games emphasized strategic planning over multiple turns, requiring players to consider long-term consequences of their actions. The complexity of these games lay in balancing economic, military, and technological development, simulating the intricacies of running a civilization.

Real-Time Strategy Breakthroughs: The RTS genre took a different approach, focusing on immediate decision-making and quick reactions. "Dune II," released in 1992, is often credited with laying the groundwork for modern RTS games. It introduced key elements such as resource gathering, base building, and direct unit control in real-time. This was followed by "Warcraft: Orcs & Humans" in 1994 and "Command & Conquer" in 1995, both of which further popularized and refined the genre. These games required players to think on their feet and adapt quickly to changing situations, combining tactical combat with strategic resource management.

The rise of RTS and TBS games represented a shift in video games towards more intellectually challenging and complex experiences. These genres appealed not just to traditional gamers but also to those who enjoyed thinking and strategy, broadening the gaming audience.

Pioneering Simulation Games and Their Real-World Impacts

The 80s and 90s also saw the emergence of simulation games, a genre dedicated to replicating real-world activities as closely as possible. These games ranged from managing cities and civilizations to simulating the experiences of flying aircraft or running a business.

City and Civilization Management: "SimCity," released in 1989, was a landmark in simulation gaming. It allowed players to design and manage a city, dealing with everything from urban planning to disaster management. This game, and its successors, influenced players' understanding of urban planning and civil engineering concepts.

Flight Simulators: The genre of flight simulation also saw significant advancements. Titles like "Microsoft Flight Simulator" provided incredibly realistic experiences of flying various aircraft. These simulators were so detailed that they were sometimes used as informal training tools for pilots.

Business and Life Simulations: Games like "Railroad Tycoon" and "The Sims" (which technically released in 2000 but was in development in the late 90s) allowed players to experience running a business or managing the daily activities of a household. These games offered insights into economics, resource management, and human behavior, making them educational as well as entertaining.

Educational Impact and Beyond: Many of these simulation games had educational impacts, teaching players about the complexities of the systems they simulated. They were used in schools and other educational settings to help illustrate real-world systems and concepts. Beyond education, they also influenced real-world fields; urban planners, for example, have noted the impact of "SimCity" on their understanding of city dynamics.

Great Strategy and Simulation Games (80s to Early 90s)

1. **SimCity (1989)** - A revolutionary city-building simulation game that introduced players to urban planning.

2. **Civilization (1991)** - A turn-based strategy game where players build and manage an empire through history.

3. **Dune II (1992)** - Often considered the first modern real-time strategy game, set in the Dune universe.

4. **Railroad Tycoon (1990)** - Combined strategy and simulation in managing a railroad empire.

5. **Warcraft: Orcs & Humans (1994)** - A foundational RTS game that set the stage for future fantasy strategy games.

6. **Populous (1989)** - An early god game that had players shaping terrain and leading followers.

7. **Sid Meier's Pirates! (1987)** - A strategy and adventure game where players live the life of a pirate.

8. **Microsoft Flight Simulator (1982)** - Began the long-running series of highly detailed flight simulation games.

9. **Command & Conquer (1995)** - A landmark RTS game known for its fast-paced gameplay and storytelling.

10. **The Settlers (1993)** - Combined resource management and strategy in a medieval setting.

11. **Lemmings (1991)** - A puzzle strategy game where players guide lemmings through various obstacles.

12. **Master of Orion (1993)** - A turn-based strategy game set in space, known for its deep gameplay.

13. **Caesar (1992)** - A city-building game set in the Roman Empire.

14. **Panzer General (1994, SSI)** - A turn-based military simulation set in World War II.

15. **Theme Park (1994)** - A simulation game where players design and manage their own theme park.

16. **Advanced Dungeons & Dragons: Pool of Radiance (1988, SSI)** - A tactical RPG with deep D&D mechanics.

17. **TIE Fighter (1994)** - A space flight simulator that let players join the Star Wars universe as a pilot.

18. **Age of Empires (1997)** - Combined real-time strategy with historical civilizations (just outside the early 90s window).

19. **Wing Commander (1990)** - A space combat simulator known for its narrative and cinematic presentation.

20. **Star Control II (1992)** - Combined space exploration, combat, and strategy elements.

21. **UFO: Enemy Unknown (X-COM: UFO Defense) (1994)** - A blend of strategy and tactical RPG elements in a sci-fi setting.

22. **Elite (1984)** - An early space trading and combat simulator, influential for its open-world design.

23. **Red Baron (1990, Dynamix)** - A flight simulator focusing on World War I aerial combat.

24. **Eye of the Beholder (1991, SSI)** - A dungeon crawler with a mix of real-time combat and RPG elements.

25. **Balance of Power (1985)** - A geopolitical simulation game focused on the Cold War era.

26. **Centurion: Defender of Rome (1990)** - Combined strategy, warfare, and chariot racing in ancient Rome.

27. **Heroes of Might and Magic (1995)** - A strategy game that combined fantasy RPG elements (slightly past the early '90s).

28. **Gold Rush! (1988, Sierra Online)** - An adventure game with strategic elements set during the California Gold Rush.

29. **F-19 Stealth Fighter (1988, MicroProse)** - A flight simulator that focused on stealth and tactical missions.

30. **Colonization (1994)** - A strategy game focused on the European colonization of the New World.

31. **Warlords (1990)** - Combined turn-based strategy and fantasy RPG elements.

32. **Gunship (1986, MicroProse)** - A helicopter combat simulator offering a realistic flying experience.

33. **Silent Service (1985, MicroProse)** - A World War II submarine simulator known for its realism.

34. **A-10 Tank Killer (1989, Dynamix)** - A flight simulator focusing on the A-10 Thunderbolt II aircraft.

35. **Powermonger (1990)** - A strategy game with a focus on conquering and managing territories.

36. **Harpoon (1989)** - A naval strategy simulation based on modern naval combat.

37. **M.U.L.E. (1983)** - An early economic simulation game set on a fictional planet.

38. **Secret Weapons of the Luftwaffe (1991, Lucasfilm Games)** - A WWII flight simulator with a focus on experimental aircraft.

39. **Romance of the Three Kingdoms (1985)** - A historical strategy game set in ancient China.

40. **Desert Strike: Return to the Gulf (1992)** - Combined strategy and action in a helicopter-based game.

41. **DragonStrike (1990, SSI)** - A flight simulator set in the Dungeons & Dragons universe.

42. **Turbo OutRun (1989)** - An arcade racing game that combined fast-paced driving with strategic elements.

43. **Shadow President (1993)** - A geopolitical simulation where players take on the role of the U.S. President.

44. **1942: The Pacific Air War (1994, MicroProse)** - A flight simulator focusing on the Pacific Theater of WWII.

45. **Falcon 3.0 (1991, Spectrum Holobyte)** - An advanced fighter jet simulator known for its realism.

46. **SimEarth (1990)** - A planetary simulation where players manage ecosystems and guide evolution.

47. **SimAnt (1991)** - Simulated the life of an ant colony, offering both educational and strategic gameplay.

48. **B-17 Flying Fortress (1992, MicroProse)** - A simulation of the famous WWII bomber, combining flight and strategy.

49. **Dungeon Master (1987)** - A dungeon crawler that combined real-time combat with strategy elements.

50. **Cruise for a Corpse (1991)** - An adventure game with strategic elements set aboard a 1920s cruise ship.

7. Racing and Sports Games

From Simple Mechanics to Realistic Simulations

The 1980s and early 1990s were transformative years for racing and sports games, marking the transition from simple, arcade-style mechanics to more realistic simulations. This evolution mirrored the technological advancements in gaming hardware, allowing for more sophisticated game designs and more authentic experiences.

Early Racing Games: Initially, racing games like "Pole Position" (1982) and "Out Run" (1986) offered basic yet thrilling experiences, focusing on high-speed gameplay and simple controls. These games typically featured third-person perspectives and emphasized speed and quick reflexes over realism.

Advancements in Racing Simulations: As technology progressed, so did the complexity and realism of racing games. Titles like "Gran Turismo" (1997), though slightly outside the early '90s window, and "F1GP" (1991) introduced detailed vehicle physics, varying weather conditions, and authentic track representations. These advancements brought the genre closer to actual driving experiences, appealing to both casual gamers and automotive enthusiasts.

Early Sports Games: In sports games, early titles like "Tecmo Bowl" (1987) and "John Madden Football" (1988) were more focused on fun and accessibility rather than accurate simulation. They offered simplified versions of the sports, making them easy to pick up and play for gamers of all skill levels.

Towards Realism in Sports Games: As the '90s progressed, sports games started to emphasize realism and accuracy. Games like "NBA Jam" (1993), while still arcade-style in gameplay, began incorporating real players and teams. Meanwhile, titles like "FIFA International Soccer" (1993) offered more realistic gameplay, mirroring the actual rules and flow of the sports they represented.

The Evolution of Multiplayer Gaming in Sports Titles

The '80s and '90s also saw significant developments in multiplayer gaming within the racing and sports genres, enhancing the competitive and social aspects of these games.

Local Multiplayer Origins: Early sports and racing games often featured local multiplayer modes, allowing friends to compete side-by-side. This was a significant draw, as it added a competitive layer to the gaming experience.

Advancements in Multiplayer Technology: With the advent of network gaming and, later, online gaming, the multiplayer experience was transformed. Though in its nascent stages in the early '90s, network gaming allowed for more complex multiplayer interactions in sports and racing games. This was a precursor to the online multiplayer experiences that would become standard in later years.

Impact on Social Gaming: These multiplayer capabilities were not just technological achievements; they also changed the social dynamic of gaming. Racing and sports games became a way for friends to connect and compete, creating shared experiences and fostering a sense of community among gamers.

Great Racing and Sports Games (80s to Early 90s)

1. **Pole Position (1982)** - An early racing game that popularized the formula of racing against the clock on a circuit.

2. **Out Run (1986)** - A seminal arcade racing game known for its fast-paced gameplay and branching paths.

3. **Tecmo Bowl (1987)** - An early American football game, beloved for its simplicity and fun multiplayer mode.

4. **Excitebike (1984)** - A motocross racing game where players could create their own tracks.

5. **John Madden Football (1988)** - Started the long-running series with its more realistic football simulation.

6. **Track & Field (1983)** - A sports-themed arcade game that tested players' speed and reflexes.

7. **Punch-Out!! (1984)** - A boxing game known for its larger-than-life characters and challenging gameplay.

8. **California Games (1987)** - Offered various outdoor sports like skateboarding and surfing in a single package.

9. **Double Dribble (1986)** - An early, influential basketball game known for its cinematic cutscenes.

10. **F1GP (1991)** - A Formula One racing simulation that offered an authentic racing experience.

11. **NBA Jam (1993)** - An over-the-top, arcade-style basketball game famous for its two-on-two gameplay.

12. **Mike Tyson's Punch-Out!! (1987)** - Featured a unique cast of characters and precise timing-based boxing mechanics.

13. **Tony Hawk's Pro Skater (1999)** - Defined the skateboarding genre with its combo-based gameplay (slightly past the early '90s).

14. **RBI Baseball (1987)** - An early baseball game known for its simplicity and accurate team rosters.

15. **Virtua Racing (1992)** - One of the first 3D racing games, offering a revolutionary visual experience.

16. **Super Monaco GP (1989)** - Combined arcade-style racing with a career mode that simulated a season of F1 racing.

17. **Hard Drivin' (1989)** - A pioneer in 3D polygonal graphics, known for its realistic driving physics.

18. **Daytona USA (1993)** - A high-speed, stock car racing game known for its multiplayer races and catchy music.

19. **FIFA International Soccer (1993)** - Offered a more realistic soccer experience with isometric gameplay.

20. **Paperboy (1984)** - A unique take on delivery and obstacle navigation in a suburban setting.

21. **Blades of Steel (1987)** - An early ice hockey game known for its fast-paced gameplay and fighting sequences.

22. **International Superstar Soccer (1994)** - Delivered a more realistic and in-depth soccer experience.

23. **SSX (2000)** - A snowboarding game offering over-the-top tricks and courses (just beyond the early '90s).

24. **Marble Madness (1984)** - A unique racing game where players navigated a marble through challenging courses.

25. **Pro Wrestling (1986)** - One of the earliest wrestling games, known for its varied move sets and characters.

26. **Sensible Soccer (1992)** - Combined simple controls with a deep gameplay experience, becoming a fan favorite.

27. **Speedball (1988)** - A futuristic sports game that mixed elements of handball and rugby with a violent twist.

28. **Road Rash (1991)** - Combined motorcycle racing with combat, known for its aggressive gameplay.

29. **Need for Speed (1994)** - Introduced realistic car handling and performance, combined with police pursuits.

30. **Cruis'n USA (1994)** - A high-speed racing game that took players across various locations in the USA.

31. **4D Sports Boxing (1991)** - One of the first 3D boxing games, offering customizable fighters and realistic physics.

32. **Wave Race (1992)** - A personal watercraft racing game known for its water physics and challenging courses.

33. **Baseball Stars (1989)** - Combined arcade-style gameplay with team management and player customization.

34. **Sega Rally Championship (1994)** - Pioneered the rally racing genre with different terrain types affecting vehicle handling.

35. **Earl Weaver Baseball (1987)** - One of the first baseball games to use real player statistics for simulation.

36. **Summer Games (1984)** - Simulated various Olympic sports, known for its multiplayer competition.

37. **Jimmy Connors Pro Tennis Tour (1991)** - Offered a realistic tennis experience with varied court surfaces and strategies.

38. **Kunio-kun no Nekketsu Soccer League (1993)** - A soccer game known for its exaggerated physics and weather effects.

39. **Winter Games (1985)** - A sports game that simulated various winter Olympic events.

40. **Skate or Die! (1987)** - A skateboarding game that offered different skateboarding events.

41. **NFL Blitz (1997)** - An arcade-style football game known for its exaggerated hits and simplified rules (just beyond the early '90s).

42. **Kick Off (1989)** - A soccer game known for its top-down view and unique ball control mechanics.

43. **World Class Track Meet (1988)** - A track and field game that used the NES Power Pad accessory.

44. **Indy 500 (1989)** - Offered a simulation of the Indianapolis 500 race with different car setups and track conditions.

45. **Arch Rivals (1989)** - A two-on-two basketball game that allowed players to punch opponents to steal the ball.

46. **Test Drive (1987)** - One of the first games to simulate driving sports cars on open roads.

47. **Virtua Tennis (1999)** - A tennis game praised for its fluid gameplay and realistic court physics (slightly past the early '90s).

48. **1080° Snowboarding (1998)** - A snowboarding game known for its realistic physics and trick system (just beyond the early '90s).

49. **ESPN Extreme Games (1995)** - Combined various extreme sports like skateboarding and mountain biking (just beyond the early '90s).

50. **Super Spike V'Ball (1989)** - A beach volleyball game known for its fast-paced gameplay and multiplayer mode.

8. Hidden Gems: Lesser-Known Titles Worth Exploring

Underrated Games with Cult Followings

The 80s and 90s were not just about the blockbuster hits; they were also a treasure trove of lesser-known titles that, over time, have garnered cult followings. These games, often overshadowed by more popular contemporaries, offered unique experiences and innovative gameplay that deserved more recognition.

Innovative Yet Overlooked: Many of these hidden gems were ahead of their time, introducing mechanics and storytelling elements that were unconventional for their era. For instance, games like "Another World" (1991) and "Flashback" (1992) offered cinematic platforming experiences with a focus on narrative and atmosphere, unlike the more traditional platformers of their time.

Cult Classics in the Making: Some games didn't receive their due during their initial release but have since been rediscovered by new generations of gamers. Titles like "Grim Fandango" (1998) and "System Shock" (1994) were not commercial hits initially but have since been recognized for their groundbreaking gameplay and storytelling.

The Appeal of the Underdog: These games often resonate with players because they offer something different from mainstream hits. Whether it's quirky gameplay, a unique art style, or an unconventional story, these hidden gems provide experiences that stand out in the crowded landscape of video game history.

The Art of Discovering Abandoned Treasures

Discovering these lesser-known titles is akin to a treasure hunt, where the reward is the rich and varied experience of gaming's past.

Exploring Abandonware Sites: Many of these hidden gems can be found on abandonware sites. These sites host games that are no longer commercially available, allowing gamers to explore titles that would otherwise be inaccessible.

Community Recommendations: Online gaming communities and forums are treasure troves of information on underrated games. Veteran gamers often share recommendations and fond memories of lesser-known titles, offering a starting point for new players to discover these games.

Retro Gaming Events: Events dedicated to retro gaming often feature exhibitions and play sessions of hidden gems. These events are not only a great way to experience these games but also to connect with a community that appreciates them.

Revisiting Old Magazines and Websites: Reading old gaming magazines or visiting archived gaming websites can provide insights into games that were overlooked at the time. These resources offer a window into the gaming culture of the past and can highlight titles that were underrated.

Hidden Gems: Lesser-Known Titles from the 80s to Early 90s

1. **Another World (1991)** - A cinematic platformer known for its narrative depth and unique art style.

2. **Flashback (1992)** - A sci-fi platformer with innovative animation and a gripping story.

3. **Grim Fandango (1998)** - A unique adventure game with a memorable story set in the afterlife (slightly past the early '90s).

4. **System Shock (1994)** - A groundbreaking action-adventure game with elements of horror and RPG.

5. **Beneath a Steel Sky (1994)** - A cyberpunk adventure game known for its compelling story and puzzles.

6. **Pathways into Darkness (1993)** - An early first-person shooter with a mix of horror and adventure elements.

7. **Syndicate (1993)** - A tactical game set in a dystopian future with deep strategic elements.

8. **Starflight (1986)** - A space exploration game combining RPG elements with a vast universe to explore.

9. **Zak McKracken and the Alien Mindbenders (1988)** - A quirky adventure game with a unique sense of humor.

10. **Little Big Adventure (1994)** - An action-adventure game with a charming story and innovative gameplay.

11. **The Lost Vikings (1992)** - A puzzle-platformer featuring three Vikings with unique abilities.

12. **Stunts (1990)** - A 3D racing game known for its track editor and physics-based gameplay.

13. **I Have No Mouth, and I Must Scream (1995)** - A dark adventure game based on Harlan Ellison's story (just beyond the early '90s).

14. **Omikron: The Nomad Soul (1999)** - An ambitious adventure game with elements of RPG, shooter, and fighting genres (slightly past the early '90s).

15. **Planescape: Torment (1999)** - An RPG with a strong narrative focus, set in the Dungeons & Dragons universe (just beyond the early '90s).

16. **Loom (1990)** - An adventure game with a unique music-based puzzle system.

17. **E.V.O.: Search for Eden (1992)** - An action platformer where players evolve through different stages of life.

18. **Descent (1994)** - A first-person shooter known for its six degrees of freedom movement.

19. **Wing Commander: Privateer (1993)** - A space trading and combat simulator set in the Wing Commander universe.

20. **Gabriel Knight: Sins of the Fathers (1993)** - A supernatural adventure game with a deep and engaging story.

21. **Sam & Max Hit the Road (1993)** - An adventure game featuring a comedic duo of freelance police.

22. **Terranigma (1995)** - An action RPG known for its intricate story and gameplay mechanics (just beyond the early '90s).

23. **Populous (1989)** - An early god game that lets players shape the land and lead their followers.

24. **Powermonger (1990)** - A strategy game focusing on conquering and managing territories.

25. **Theme Hospital (1997)** - A humorous hospital management simulation game (just beyond the early '90s).

26. **Dungeon Keeper (1997)** - A strategy game where players build and manage a dungeon (just beyond the early '90s).

27. **Alone in the Dark (1992)** - A survival horror game that influenced future games in the genre.

28. **Harvester (1996)** - A point-and-click adventure game known for its bizarre and disturbing content (just beyond the early '90s).

29. **The 7th Guest (1993)** - An interactive movie puzzle adventure game with a horror theme.

30. **Rise of the Dragon (1990)** - A cyberpunk adventure game with a noir detective story.

31. **Darklands (1992)** - A historical fantasy RPG set in medieval Germany.

32. **Anvil of Dawn (1995)** - A dungeon crawler known for its immersive world and storytelling (just beyond the early '90s).

33. **NetHack (1987)** - A classic ASCII roguelike game known for its depth and complexity.

34. **Blackthorne (1994)** - A cinematic platformer with a focus on action and puzzle-solving.

35. **Colonization (1994)** - A strategy game about the European colonization of the Americas.

36. **Master of Magic (1994)** - A 4X strategy game combining elements of magic and fantasy.

37. **Betrayal at Krondor (1993)** - An RPG that blended storytelling with a vast open world.

38. **The Bard's Tale (1985)** - An influential RPG with deep dungeon crawling elements.

39. **Myst (1993)** - A graphic adventure puzzle game known for its stunning visuals and immersive gameplay.

40. **Heretic (1994)** - A fantasy-themed first-person shooter using the Doom engine.

41. **Shadow of the Comet (1993)** - An adventure game inspired by the works of H.P. Lovecraft.

42. **Pirates! Gold (1993)** - A remake of the original "Pirates!" game, offering improved graphics and gameplay.

43. **Indiana Jones and the Fate of Atlantis (1992)** - An adventure game that captures the spirit of the Indiana Jones films.

44. **The Dig (1995)** - A science-fiction adventure game based on an idea by Steven Spielberg (just beyond the early '90s).

45. **The Oregon Trail (1990 version)** - An educational game simulating the life of pioneers on the Oregon Trail.

46. **SimTower (1994)** - A simulation game focused on building and managing a skyscraper.

47. **Beneath a Steel Sky (1994)** - A cyberpunk adventure game with a compelling narrative.

48. **Day of the Tentacle (1993)** - A time-travel adventure game known for its humor and unique art style.

49. **The Incredible Machine (1993)** - A puzzle game where players create complex machines to solve challenges.

50. **Ultima Underworld: The Stygian Abyss (1992)** - A first-person RPG known for its immersive world and innovative gameplay.

9. Preserving the Past: The Role of Emulators and Communities

Legal and Ethical Aspects of Emulation

The practice of emulation, which involves using software or hardware to replicate the functionality of older gaming systems on modern devices, plays a critical role in preserving the history of video gaming. However, this practice also raises important legal and ethical considerations.

Legal Challenges: The primary legal issue with emulation is copyright infringement. Most vintage games are still protected under copyright law, meaning that distributing or downloading them without permission is technically illegal, even if the games are no longer commercially available. Emulators themselves, when not using proprietary code, are generally legal, but the ROMs (the game files) often are not unless explicitly released or licensed by the copyright holder.

Ethical Considerations: From an ethical standpoint, many argue that emulation is vital for preserving gaming history, especially when original hardware and software are no longer available or functional. Emulators allow current and future generations to experience classic games, keeping the games alive in the public consciousness. The ethical debate often hinges on the difference between preservation and piracy, with many advocates arguing that emulation serves a valuable cultural and historical purpose.

How Online Communities Keep Abandonware Alive

Abandonware refers to software that is no longer sold or supported by its original creator. Many classic games fall into this category, and online communities play a crucial role in keeping these games accessible.

Sharing Knowledge and Resources: Online communities dedicated to retro gaming often share information on how to run old games on modern systems, provide support for emulation and troubleshooting, and sometimes offer downloads of abandonware games. These communities are invaluable resources for both new players looking to explore classic titles and veteran gamers seeking to revisit games from their past.

Creating Mods and Updates: In some cases, enthusiasts in these communities create mods, updates, and patches for older games, improving compatibility with modern hardware or adding new features to classic titles. This not only preserves the original games but can also breathe new life into them.

Documenting and Archiving: Beyond just sharing games, these communities often document the history of video gaming, archiving manuals, artwork, and other materials related to classic games. This documentation is crucial for preserving the broader context and culture surrounding these games.

Advocacy for Legal Recognition: Some community members advocate for legal recognition of the importance of preserving digital gaming history. They call for changes in copyright law to recognize the value of preserving old games as cultural artifacts, arguing that this is essential for future historical and academic work.

10. The Legacy and Future of Abandonware

Influence on Modern Game Design

Abandonware, referring to older games no longer supported or sold by their developers, has had a significant impact on modern game design. These classic titles often serve as a blueprint for contemporary game development, influencing both the mechanics and storytelling of new games.

Learning from the Past: Many modern game designers grew up playing these classic games, drawing inspiration from their innovative gameplay and narrative techniques. The simplicity yet depth found in older games, such as the puzzle-solving of "Myst" or the branching narratives in early RPGs, continue to influence current game design philosophies.

Revival of Classic Genres: There's a noticeable trend in the gaming industry where classic genres, once thought to be obsolete, are being revived and modernized. For instance, the recent resurgence of point-and-click adventure games and pixel art styles in indie games is a direct homage to the classics of the 80s and 90s.

Adapting Old Mechanics for New Technologies: Modern games often incorporate mechanics first pioneered in older titles, adapting and evolving them to fit new technologies and gaming platforms. This includes everything from the complex strategy elements of early RTS games to the narrative-driven exploration of classic adventure games.

The Continued Appeal of Retro Gaming

Despite the advancements in graphics and gameplay mechanics, retro gaming maintains a strong appeal, both to those who experienced these games when they were new and to younger gamers discovering them for the first time.

Nostalgia Factor: For many, retro games evoke a sense of nostalgia, offering a window back to childhood or teenage years. This emotional connection is a powerful draw, leading many gamers to seek out and play abandonware titles.

Simplicity and Charm: There's an allure to the simplicity and straightforwardness of older games. The pixel art, chiptune music, and less complex gameplay of retro games have a unique charm that stands in contrast to the often overwhelming complexity of modern titles.

Discovery and Preservation: For newer generations, retro games represent a chance to explore the history of the medium. This sense of discovery, coupled with efforts to preserve gaming history, adds to the appeal of abandonware. Gaming enthusiasts and historians alike recognize the importance of these games in understanding the evolution of gaming as both a technology and an art form.

Community Engagement: Online communities centered around retro gaming and abandonware continue to thrive. These communities not only share games but also experiences, memories, and modifications, creating a vibrant culture around these classic titles.

11. Appendix: Resources and How to Play

A Guide to Safe and Legal Abandonware Gaming

Exploring the world of abandonware can be a thrilling journey into gaming history, but it's important to navigate this landscape safely and legally.

Understanding Legal Implications: While abandonware is not supported by its original developers or publishers, it doesn't always mean it's legally free to use. It's essential to understand the copyright status of a game before downloading it. Some developers have released their old games for free, making them legally available.

Using Trusted Sources: When looking for abandonware games, use reputable websites. Trusted sites often offer a library of games that are legally free to download. Be cautious of sites that may host pirated software or contain malicious content.

Respecting Copyright Laws: Always respect copyright laws. If a game is not explicitly stated as free by the rights holder, assume it's still protected under copyright law. Seek out games that have been released into the public domain or have been abandoned by their developers without any legal claim.

Recommended Emulators and Tools

To play older games on modern systems, you'll often need emulators and other tools. Here's a list of some of the most popular and user-friendly options:

1. **DOSBox:** An emulator for running DOS-based games. It's widely used for playing classic PC games from the 80s and early 90s.

2. **ScummVM:** Perfect for playing old point-and-click adventure games, ScummVM is designed to run games that use the SCUMM engine (like many LucasArts classics).

3. **MAME (Multiple Arcade Machine Emulator):** Ideal for playing old arcade games, MAME emulates a vast array of arcade games from different eras.

4. **RetroArch:** A versatile emulator that can run games from consoles like the NES, SNES, Genesis, and many more. It's a frontend for various emulators, offering a unified interface for playing games from different platforms.

5. **ePSXe:** A PlayStation emulator that allows you to play PS1 games on your PC. It's known for its high compatibility and performance.

6. **VisualBoyAdvance:** A highly recommended emulator for playing Game Boy, Game Boy Color, and Game Boy Advance games.

7. **PCSX2:** For those interested in PlayStation 2 games, PCSX2 is one of the best emulators available for that console.

8. **OpenEmu (for Mac):** An emulator specifically designed for macOS, OpenEmu offers an easy-to-use interface and supports a wide range of console games.

Using ROMs and Disk Images: Remember, the emulator is just a tool to run the game. You'll also need ROMs or disk images of the games you want to play. Only download ROMs of games that you legally own or that are freely available from the copyright holder.

Backing Up Your Own Games: If you own a physical copy of a game, you can create a digital backup (such as a ROM or ISO file) for personal use. Tools like disk imaging software can help you make these backups.

12. Conclusion: The Timeless Appeal of 80s and 90s Games

Reflections on the Cultural Impact

The games of the 1980s and 1990s were more than just entertainment; they were cultural milestones that shaped an entire generation. Reflecting on the cultural impact of these games reveals their significant role in not just the world of gaming, but in broader pop culture as well.

Beyond Gaming: These decades saw video games evolve from simple diversions to complex narratives that could rival films and books. Iconic characters like Mario and Sonic became cultural icons, recognizable far beyond the gaming community. The storytelling, art, and music of these games influenced other media, inspiring movies, music, and literature.

Shaping Social Interactions: These games also played a role in shaping social interactions among gamers. Arcades became social hubs, and later, multiplayer games fostered connections and friendships, some lasting decades. The rise of competitive gaming and the emergence of gaming communities around certain titles fostered a sense of belonging and shared identity.

Technological Innovation: The 80s and 90s were a hotbed of technological innovation in gaming, from the transition from 8-bit to 16-bit and beyond, to the advent of 3D graphics. These technological leaps were not just milestones in gaming history; they also pushed the boundaries of what was possible in digital entertainment.

The Ongoing Journey of Rediscovery in Gaming

The journey of rediscovering 80s and 90s games is ongoing, as new generations of gamers explore these classics.

Preservation and Accessibility: The efforts to preserve and make these games accessible are crucial in keeping this part of gaming history alive. Emulators, online communities, and legal re-releases allow new players to experience these games and appreciate their historical significance.

Learning from the Past: Modern game developers and designers continue to draw inspiration from these classics, learning from their design principles and storytelling techniques. The success of retro-inspired games and remakes/remasters is a testament to the enduring appeal of the gameplay and aesthetics of this era.

A Timeless Legacy: The games of the 80s and 90s have a timeless appeal. They remind us of a simpler time in gaming, where creativity and innovation were driven by the limits of technology. They offer a window into the past, not just for nostalgic enjoyment, but as a reminder of how far the gaming industry has come and where it might go next.

In conclusion, the games of the 80s and 90s hold a special place in the history of gaming and popular culture. Their impact extends far beyond their original release, influencing modern game design, technology, and culture. As we continue to rediscover and preserve these games, we ensure that their legacy endures, not just as relics of the past but as living, influential pieces of cultural history.

Appendix: Unique and Overlooked Games from the 80s to Early 90s

1. **Marathon (1994)** - An early first-person shooter known for its deep storyline and large, non-linear levels.

2. **Robotron: 2084 (1982)** - A fast-paced twin-stick shooter with a simple premise and addictive gameplay.

3. **Jazz Jackrabbit (1994)** - A fast-paced platformer featuring a green rabbit with attitude and futuristic weapons.

4. **The Oregon Trail (1990 edition)** - An educational adventure game simulating pioneer life on the Oregon Trail.

5. **Elite (1984)** - A pioneering open-world space exploration and trading game with groundbreaking 3D graphics.

6. **Star Control II (1992)** - A space exploration game combining strategy, ship combat, and resource management.

7. **Maniac Mansion (1987)** - A groundbreaking point-and-click adventure game with multiple possible endings.

8. **Lemmings (1991)** - A puzzle game where players guide lemmings through various obstacles.

9. **Carmen Sandiego series (1985-1994)** - A series of educational mystery games focusing on geography and history.

10. **The Hitchhiker's Guide to the Galaxy (1984)** - A text adventure game based on Douglas Adams' famous book.

11. **Zork series (1980-1994)** - A classic series of text adventure games known for their rich storytelling.

12. **SimEarth (1990)** - A simulation game where players control the development of a planet.

13. **Sid Meier's Pirates! (1987)** - A pirate-themed strategy/adventure game where players sail the high seas.

14. **Prince of Persia (1989)** - A platformer known for its fluid animation and time-limited gameplay.

15. **Myst (1993)** - A graphic adventure puzzle game known for its stunning visuals and immersive gameplay.

16. **Oregon Trail II (1995)** - An expanded and updated version of the classic educational game (just beyond the early '90s).

17. **Stunts (1990)** - A 3D racing game known for its track editor and physics-based gameplay.

18. **Starflight (1986)** - A space exploration game combining RPG elements with a vast universe to explore.

19. **The 7th Guest (1993)** - An interactive movie puzzle adventure game with a horror theme.

20. **Colonization (1994)** - A strategy game about the European colonization of the Americas.

21. **Beneath a Steel Sky (1994)** - A cyberpunk adventure game with a compelling narrative.

22. **Day of the Tentacle (1993)** - A time-travel adventure game known for its humor and unique art style.

23. **The Incredible Machine (1993)** - A puzzle game where players create complex machines to solve challenges.

24. **Archon: The Light and the Dark (1983)** - A strategy game that blends chess-like planning with real-time combat.

25. **Tass Times in Tonetown (1986)** - An adventure game set in a bizarre, punk-inspired alternate universe.

26. **A Mind Forever Voyaging (1985)** - A text-based science fiction game with a focus on exploration and narrative.

27. **Ultima Underworld: The Stygian Abyss (1992)** - A first-person RPG known for its immersive world and innovative gameplay.

28. **Dungeon Master (1987)** - A dungeon crawler that combined real-time combat with strategy elements.

29. **R-Type (1987)** - A side-scrolling shooter known for its difficulty and unique power-up system.

30. **Shadowgate (1987)** - A fantasy adventure game famous for its challenging puzzles and atmospheric storytelling.

31. **Deja Vu (1985)** - A noir adventure game with a unique interface and detective story.

32. **Wasteland (1988)** - A post-apocalyptic RPG that inspired the Fallout series.

33. **King's Quest series (1984-1994)** - A series of adventure games known for their storytelling and puzzle-solving.

34. **Police Quest series (1987-1993)** - Adventure games that simulate the experience of being a police officer.

35. **The Bard's Tale series (1985-1991)** - A series of fantasy RPGs known for their challenging gameplay and humor.

36. **Adventure Construction Set (1985)** - Allowed players to create their own graphical adventure games.

37. **SimAnt (1991)** - Simulated the life of an ant colony, offering both educational and strategic gameplay.

38. **Phantasy Star II (1989)** - A groundbreaking RPG with a deep narrative and complex gameplay.

39. **Uninvited (1986)** - A point-and-click adventure game with a horror theme.

40. **Defender of the Crown (1986)** - A strategy game set in medieval England with various gameplay elements.

41. **The Secret of Monkey Island (1990)** - A defining game in the adventure genre with its pirate theme and humor.

42. **Zombies Ate My Neighbors (1993)** - A quirky run-and-gun game with a focus on rescuing neighbors from monsters.

43. **Turrican II (1991)** - An action-packed platformer known for its expansive levels and smooth gameplay.

44. **M.U.L.E. (1983)** - An early economic simulation game set on a fictional planet.

45. **Kings of the Beach (1988)** - A beach volleyball game known for its gameplay and multiplayer mode.

46. **Streets of Rage 2 (1992)** - A beat 'em up game known for its soundtrack and cooperative gameplay.

47. **Wings (1990)** - A World War I flight simulation game with a mix of action and narrative.

48. **Lode Runner (1983)** - A puzzle-platformer where players collect gold while avoiding enemies.

49. **Blaster Master (1988)** - Combined platforming and run-and-gun gameplay with vehicle sections.

50. **Earthworm Jim (1994)** - A platformer known for its humor, unique character design, and challenging gameplay.

Appendix: Ode to Abandonware

In realms of bytes and circuit's lore,
Lies the trove of yesteryear's core,
Abandonware, the forgotten script,
In digital crypts, silently kept.

Once heralded in arcade's bright hall,
Now echoes in memory's gallant call,
Sprites and pixels, in colors arrayed,
In the hearts of players, forever stayed.

Oh noble quests and dungeons deep,
Where heroes' vows were sworn to keep,
In the land of might and magic's reign,
Their valorous deeds, not in vain.

Cartridges and floppy disks, in dust they bide,
Yet in our minds, they vividly reside,
From the clatter of keys, adventures unfold,
In these tales, the past's secrets told.

Space odysseys 'cross the starlit expanse,
Where galaxies in pixel dances prance,
In code and cipher, their fates were cast,
In the cosmos of the digital vast.

Fantasy realms, dragons' lair,
Echoes of battle, through the air,
Elves and mages, in fellowship bound,
In the bits of yore, their legends found.

Racing through pixelated lanes,
Where once we steered, memory remains,
Speed and thrill, the engine's roar,
In circuits' maze, forevermore.

Of kingdoms lost and treasures rare,
Of pirate's cove and maiden fair,
In the machine's deep, silent sleep,
These ancient stories, secrets keep.

So let us honor these games of old,
Their tales in whispered reverence told,
For in abandonware's forgotten trove,
Lies the youth we dearly wove.

In virtual worlds, our spirits soared,
By binary bards and code conjured,
In the shadow of progress's relentless march,
In these games, our past's eternal arch.